D0913943

What Does the President Do?

By Amanda Miller

Children's Press®
An Imprint of Scholastic Inc.
New York Toronto London Auckland Sydney
Mexico City New Delhi Hong Kong
Danbury, Connecticut

These content vocabulary word builders are for grades 1–2.

Subject Consultant: Eli J. Lesser, MA, Director of Education, National Constitution Center, Philadelphia, Pennsylvania

Reading Consultant: Cecilia Minden-Cupp, PhD, Early Literacy Consultant and Author, Chapel Hill, North Carolina

Photographs © 2009: Alamy Images/David R. Frazier Photolibrary, Inc.: 4 top, 14; AP Images: 21 right (M.Spencer Green), 19 top right (Doug Mills); Corbis Images: 5 top left, 16 right (Rick Barrentine), 1, 11 top (Bettmann), 17 (Joyce N. Boghosian), 11 bottom (Gary Hershorn/Reuters), back cover, 4 bottom left, 8 (Brooks Kraft), 4 bottom right, 10 (Kevin Lamarque/Reuters), 20 left (Reuters), 19 top left (Stanley Tetrick/Sygma); Getty Images: cover background (Peter Gridley), 13 (Marc Hall), 21 left (Ron Hoskins/NBAE), 23 top right (Uyen Le), 5 top right, 16 left (Paul J. Richards/AFP), 2, 9 (Joe Sohm/Visions of America), 20 right (Chip Somodevilla); iStockphoto/Julia Nichols: 23 top left; NEWSCOM/Chris Kleponis/ AFP: 15; PhotoEdit/David Frazier: 23 bottom right; Redux Pictures: 19 bottom (Paul Hosefros/The New York Times), 7 (Ozier Muhammad/The New York Times); Courtesy of Ronald Reagan Presidential Library: 5 bottom left, 12; Superstock, Inc./Purestock: 23 bottom left; Courtesy of the U.S. Senate: cover foreground. Maps by James McMahon

Series Design: Simonsays Design!
Art Direction, Production, and Digital Imaging: Scholastic Classroom Magazines

Library of Congress Cataloging-in-Publication Data

Miller, Amanda, 1974-
What Does the President Do? / Amanda Miller.
p. cm. – (Scholastic news nonfiction readers)
Includes bibliographical references and index.
ISBN 13: 978-0-531-21088-8 (lib. bidg.) 978-0-531-22425-0 (pbk.)
ISBN 10: 0-531-21088-X (lib. bdg.) 0-531-22425-2 (pbk.)
1. Presidents–United States–Juvenile literature. 2. Political leadership–United States--Juvenile literature. 3. Executive power–United States–Juvenile literature. 4. United States–Politics and government–Decision making–Juvenile literature. I. Title.
JK517.M55 2009
352.230973–dc22 2008028624

Published simultaneously in Canada. Printed in China.

4 5 6 7 8 9 10 R 18 17 16 15 14 13 12 11 62

CONTENTS

Word Hunt 4–5

What Does the President Do? 6–7

The White House 8–9

Helping to Make Laws 10–11

Giving Speeches 12–13

Meeting with Leaders 14–15

Head of the Military 16–17

Having Fun 18–19

Meet President Barack Obama 20–21

Your New Words 22

Ways We Remember Our First President, George Washington 23

Index 24

Find Out More 24

Meet the Author 24

WORD HUNT

Look for these words as you read. They will be in **bold**.

Air Force One
(air forss wuhn)

Oval Office
(**oh**-vuhl **off**-iss)

signs
(sines)

medal
(**med**-uhl)

military
(**mil**-uh-tair-ee)

speech
(speech)

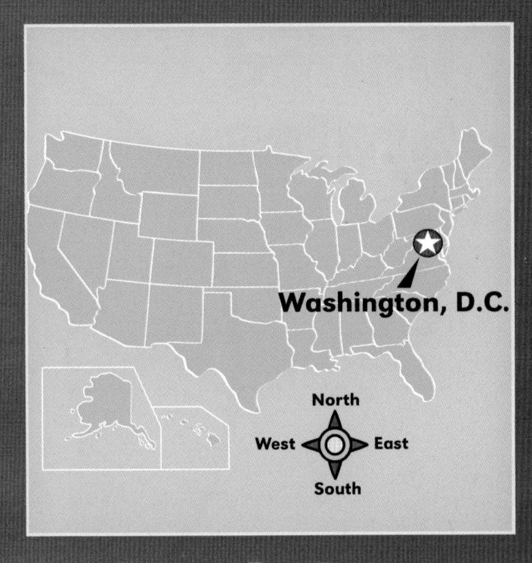

United States
(yoo-**nye**-ted states)

What Does the President Do?

The President is the leader of the **United States**. We vote for a new President every four years. It is a big job!

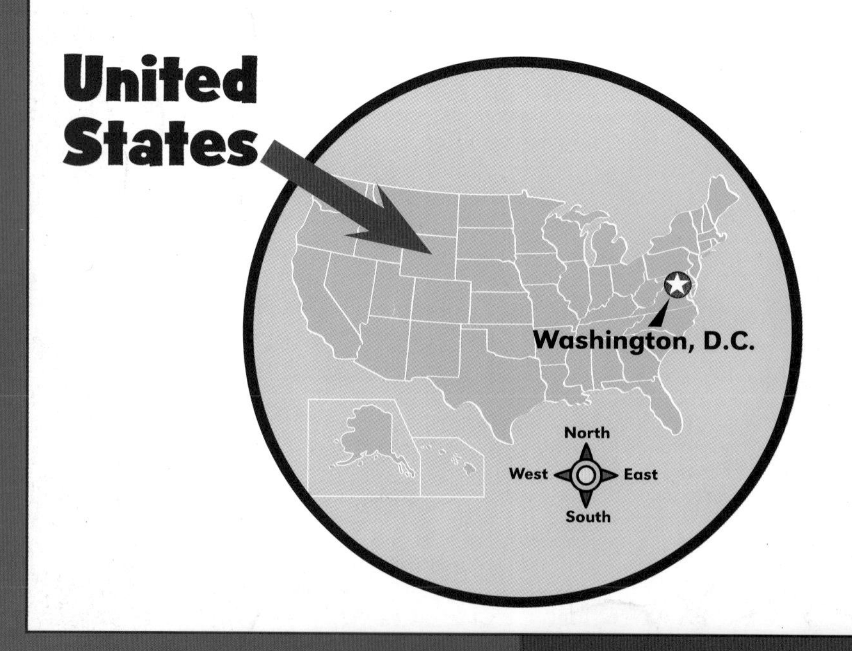

Barack Obama became President in 2009. He is our 44th President.

The President works and lives in a big house. It is called the White House.

The room where the President works is called the **Oval Office**. It really is shaped like an oval!

The White House is in Washington, D.C., our country's capital.

The President helps to make laws. Laws are rules for our country.

Laws are written on paper that the President **signs**.

President Johnson and President Bush helped make laws for everyone to follow.

Have you ever seen the President give a **speech** on TV? The President gives many speeches, or talks. The speeches tell us what is happening in our country.

People all over the country listen when the President gives a speech.

The President meets with leaders from other countries. They talk about ways to work together.

The President flies to other countries on a huge plane. It is called **Air Force One**.

dent Clinton met with the leader
ngladesh [BANG-luh-desh].

The President is also the leader of the U.S. **military**. The President decides how the military will keep us safe.

Sometimes the President gives a **medal** for a job well done!

President George W. Bush gave this soldier a medal.

The President does not work all the time. There are sometimes big parties at the White House. Family time is also important to the President.

The President works hard but has fun too!

President Kennedy and his son.

President Carter and Mrs. Carter.

Dancers at a White House celebration.

MEET PRESIDENT

- President Obama was born in Hawaii.
- His wife's name is Michelle.
- He has two daughters, named Malia and Sasha.

BARACK OBAMA

★ He likes playing basketball.

★ He likes cooking chili.

★ He has written two books.

★ Before he was President, he was a Senator from Illinois.

YOUR NEW WORDS

Air Force One (air forss wuhn) the plane on which the President flies

medal (**med**-uhl) a piece of metal on a ribbon. A medal is given to someone for being brave or for helping his or her country.

military (**mil**-uh-tair-ee) the people who fight for and protect a country, such as members of the Army or Navy

Oval Office (**oh**-vuhl **off**-iss) the President's office in the White House

signs (sines) When you sign something, you write your name in your own way.

speech (speech) a talk to a group of people

United States (yoo-**nye**-ted states) a nation of 50 states in North America

WAYS WE REMEMBER OUR FIRST PRESIDENT, GEORGE WASHINGTON

The Dollar Bill

The Washington Monument

Mount Rushmore

Washington, D.C.

INDEX

Air Force One, 4, 14

families, 18

laws, 10

medals, 5, 16
military, 5, 16

Obama, Barack, 7, 20-21
Obama, Malia, 20
Obama, Michelle, 20
Obama, Sasha, 20
Oval Office, 4, 8

parties, 18

signing, 4, 10
speeches, 5, 12

United States, 5, 6

voting, 6

White House, 8, 18

FIND OUT MORE

Book:

Buller, Jon; Schade, Susan; and Weber, Jill. *Smart About the Presidents.* New York: Grosset and Dunlap, 2004.

Website:

http://pbskids.org/wayback/prez/index.html

MEET THE AUTHOR

Amanda Miller is a writer and editor for Scholastic. She and her dog, Henry, live in Brooklyn, New York.